A Dog's Day

by Ava Bennett
illustrated by Tina Innes

Practice Pre-Decodable 1

McGraw Hill Education

Bothell, WA • Chicago, IL • Columbus, OH • New York, NY

MHEonline.com

Send all inquiries to:
McGraw-Hill Education
8787 Orion Place
Columbus, OH 43240

ISBN: 978-0-02-140896-2
MHID: 0-02-140896-3

Printed in China.

9 10 11 12 13 DSS 27 26 25 24 23